Miracles
Inspiring Stories
of Hope

MIRACLES by Lynn Valentine

Published by PREMIUM PRESS AMERICA

Copyright © 2001 by Lynn Valentine

ISBN 1-887654-77-1

Library of Congress Catalog Card Number 00 133633

PREMIUM PRESS AMERICA gift books are available at special discounts for premiums, sales promotions, fund-raising, or educational use. For details contact the Publisher at P.O. Box 159015, Nashville, TN 37215, or phone toll free (800) 891-7323 or (615)256-8484, or fax us at (615)256-8624.

For more information visit our web site at *www.premiumpress.com*.

Editor Mardy Fones
Cover and Interior Design by Bob Bubnis/BookSetters—bksetters@aol.com
Cover photo: "Ascension" by Dave Staniforth

First Edition 2001
2 3 4 5 6 7 8 9 10

Miracles
Inspiring Stories of Hope

by
Lynn Valentine

PREMIUM PRESS AMERICA
NASHVILLE, TENNESSEE

mir·a·cle, n. a wonder; supernatural event.

Dedication

I would first like to dedicate this book to My Guardian Angels for helping me see the miracles in my own life. I thank them for the miraculous way they deliver messages—for the healing touch my heart receives when I need it most—and for the gentle pat on the back when I do the right thing. Thank you for watching over me.

I would also like to dedicate this work to Rich Mullins. Your music changed my life and caused me to chase after God. Without you I might not have ever seen the miracle in the color green. I miss you.

"There are two ways to live your life.
One is as though nothing is a miracle.
The other is as though everything is a miracle."
— Albert Einstein

Table of Contents

MIRACLES

Introduction

*F*or so many years I have seen miracles with unopened eyes. It was only through meeting those who felt in their hearts, the need to share their own miracles, that I understood what I already knew—that God is with us, and working around us always.

Before writing this book, I felt a miracle had to be something huge like another parting of the Red Sea. All that changed and I am no longer blinded by my own near-sightedness.

The stories you will read here are the stories of true miracles. Sometimes they are as big as a rockslide, and sometimes they are as subtle as a baby in a manger. Through the generosity of those who shared their stories, I have learned to look for the miracles in my life too. Whether big or small, they are all still miracles and in seeing them, I see God and His Angels Everywhere.

Blessings, Love and Peace,

Lynn Valentine

Lynn Valentine

Power of Prayer

A missionary on leave told this true story while visiting his home church in Michigan.

"While in Africa, I served in a small field hospital. Part of my duties there involved traveling by bicycle every two weeks to pick up supplies. This was quite a trip though, and took two full days to make, so, midway between the hospital and the town, I would find a place to camp out overnight.

"On one of these trips, I stopped by the bank to get some money and then picked up the medicine and supplies that were on my list when I saw two men fighting. By the time I made my way to the center of things, the fight had ended leaving one man on the ground seriously hurt. I treated his injuries and, as I was bandaging him up, I talked to him about Jesus. When I had done all I could and was certain he would be okay, I got on my bike, took my two-day trip and arrived safely back at the hospital, forgetting about the entire episode.

"The next month came and again, I did my supply run. When I got back to the city, I was happy to see the young man I had treated, looking much better than he had the last time I saw him.

"He seemed to have something important to tell me, so I stopped and sat with him. He told me that while I was taking care of him, he noticed that I was carrying money and medicines with me. He said that in spite of my goodness to him, he and some friends had plotted together to follow me into the jungle and overtake me in the night. 'We planned to kill you and take your money and drugs, but just as we went to your camp, we saw that you were surrounded by 26 armed guards.'

"I was confused as I always travelled alone. I laughed at the notion of being escorted by armed guards. The young man persisted though, insisting that he and his five friends had counted them, before becoming afraid and leaving the camp site."

At this point in the missionary's message, one of the men in the congregation stood up and interrupted. After asking the missionary when this took place, the man in the pew began telling the rest of the story. . .

"On the night this happened to you in Africa, it was morning here and I was getting ready to go play golf. While I was out on the course, I felt a sudden and strong urge to pray for you. In fact, the feeling was so intense that I called others in the church and had them meet with me to pray for you."

He then turned to the congregation and asked all the men who came to pray, to stand up.

There were 26.

—Anonymous

"The angel of the Lord encamps around those who fear him, and he delivers them."

—Psalm 34:7 NIV

The Hand of God

About five years ago, my family was going through an extremely difficult time. My husband was having trouble at work and the children were having trouble at school. Ours was an unhappy household. I tried to the best of my ability to get over this rough spot to no avail.

Late one night, I couldn't sleep. I was up roaming through the house trying to think of something that would alleviate my family's anguish. I asked God to please help with this situation that had us all down. I suddenly got an idea of writing little sayings and leaving them in a highly visible spot in the house that would serve as an inspiration for the family. I had about 15 of these sayings that flooded into my mind. I knew it was God that had given me that idea. I thanked Him as I jotted them down and went to bed.

The next day, I was going to put that idea into service. I looked at my first saying and was attempting to write it on the paper, but couldn't. I have had MS for nearly 15 years and it affects my writing hand. I haven't been able to write in nearly 10 years. I couldn't even hold the pen in my hand. I was so discouraged.

I said to God, "This was your idea. You do the writing."

I again took the pen and held it to the paper. I began writing this beautiful script. I felt no pressure on my hand as if it were being guided. I couldn't even feel the pen in my hand. Despite my medical condition, I was holding the pen and writing more beautifully than I ever had written in my life. It was awesome.

I taped the paper to the entry way so the family could see it when they came home. Everyone asked who wrote it and my reply to them was, "God". It worked! Everyday I would write a new saying and the family began looking forward to seeing the paper hanging there. In time, our spirits were lifted and things began running more smoothly again.

After I had exhausted the initial 15 sayings, I decided that since the family liked it so well, I would just continue with it. I made up one of my own and was attempting to write it down but I just couldn't. I couldn't even hold the pen. It was over. It was done.

God had answered my prayer. He gave me the idea and He wrote the sayings. I wrote with the Hand of God.

—Lauren C.

It's Me, Daniel

*T*wo years ago, I was watching a talk show; the guests were authors of a book on angels. At the time, I had no real religious convictions and thought the whole idea was silly.

Nevertheless, two days later, I found myself laying in bed and thinking about the show. I remember really being preoccupied with what I had heard, and imagined an angel being around me. I started talking to him and although I am sure it seems silly, I began referring to my imagined angel as "Daniel."

The next day I went to run some errands and upon my return found two messages on my recorder. One from my husband, and one that said

"Hi, it's me Daniel. Call me." I thought it was a wrong number, and deleted it but later remembered the experience the night before with the angel thoughts I was having.

From that moment on, I began to read books on angels and began to consider "Daniel" to be my constant companion.

Not long after that, there was a huge hurricane in the Caribbean. My mother had a house right there in the path of the storm and my fear grew as the strength of the hurricane grew to a category five.

I remember praying, asking God to please bless my mother's home. That night, as I was going to sleep I felt a pressure over my body. It was almost as if the air was heavy over me. I then felt a soft wind in my ear and I heard a voice tell me not to worry; that the hurricane would hit the island but that He would blow it over my mother's house; I remember my hair moved gently as the voice spoke.

The storm hit and the devastation was massive. Because phone lines were out, there was no way to communicate with the islands. All we could do was wait. Ten long days went by before we finally got the news that while the surrounding villages and towns had been hit hard, the hurricane seemed to have just skipped over the town where Mom lived.

I remembered the message my angel delivered and smiled. Sure it went over her house, Daniel said it would!

—*Blanca Greenberg*

Ceiling Fan Rescue

*I*t was a hot summer afternoon in Texas around 14 years ago. My son was just a year old at the time and running a very high fever. We had already gone to the doctor who blamed it on a flu and told us to keep him resting. This was not a problem as he was so sick that he couldn't move. He was so out of it that he wouldn't even sit up.

As this was the first time he had been sick, I stayed with him every second, placing a quilt under the ceiling fan with some pillows and laid down on the floor with him to watch television. After he had been asleep for some time, I decided to get up and get a little done around the house.

I had only left the room for three or four seconds, making it a short ways down the hall, when I heard a terrible crashing noise. I spun around running into the living room to see the ceiling fan had fallen to the ground and was a heap of metal, wood and shattered glass on the quilt.

MY BABY!!!

Before I got to the quilt, my eyes went to the sofa where my baby sat, crying softly. I was in shock. He should have been under the heavy ceiling fan, but was sitting on the couch. He was sound asleep when I left, weak with fever, and yet only a few seconds later, he was on the couch.

There was no way he could have gotten up and made it to the couch in the few seconds I was gone. I am convinced that when I left, an angel moved him to safety.

Today, he is 15, and while mothers always worry about their children, it is comforting to know that their guardian angels watch out for them too.

—*Kristi Judd*

Faith is telling a mountain to move
and being shocked only when it doesn't.

Mountain Moving Miracle

I was coming down a tall ladder when the worst thing happened. Somehow, it became unstable and began to slowly tilt. Powerless to stop it, I braced myself for the fall.

Although I really didn't experience that much pain at first, it turned out that I broke my humerus bone, my pelvis, a vertebra, my left wrist and left heel. They operated on me the next day and told me to expect to spend three months in hospital rehab and another three months in a wheelchair.

Before the accident, I had been studying Mark 11:23-24. It is all about trusting and having absolute faith in God. "*Truthfully, I say to you, who ever shall say to that mountain, be removed and cast into the sea, if there is no doubt in his heart, and believes it will come to pass, he shall see it happen. So, whatever you desire, and pray for, believe that you will receive it and you will."*

At the time, I had been praying about my eyesight which was very poor. Now though, laying in the hospital bed, I had a longer list of body parts that needed healing, but I also had a lot of time to pray about it too. If it were God's will that I be healed, then all that was needed now was for me to believe it.

So I prayed, thanking Him in advance for my healing, and believed it. As I thanked Him, a profound warming like I had never felt before went into my bones. It lasted for only a couple of seconds then I fell asleep. I awoke at 3 A.M. to a tingling in the left side of my body. I raised my knee to my chest, with no problem in my pelvis, I moved my back and where it once felt weakened by the broken vertebrae, if felt fine now. When I went back for x-rays, the doctor could not believe it. He called in the original x-rays to compare them with the new shots. Clear breaks in the bones were easily seen in the old ones, but no trace of a break could be found in the new ones.

I was walking in two weeks, and in four weeks I was back home, getting around great.

As I gave thanks to God, I began to notice that I could see much better too. I went to my ophthalmologist whom I had been seeing for the past 20 years, and had myself tested. He, too, was baffled.

"Ted, I have never seen your eyes in better shape than they are now. You are reading characters on the 20/25 scale!" I had been wearing glasses since I was two years old, but now, I didn't need them.

Why doesn't everyone get healed like that? I don't know, but I do believe that the reason I was put back together again was so that I could tell you this story now. May it bless you and always help you remember that His grace is sufficient, and that if you do jump (or fall) into His arms, He will catch you!

—Ted R. Jefferies

Miracle Baby

*L*ittle Trevor was born after 31 hours of labor. To deliver him, the doctor had to dislocate both of his shoulders. Trevor barely breathed and no cry was heard when he came into the world.

The nurses rushed him quickly away to put him under oxygen and the parents were left with no options except to pray.

I was a close family friend, so when they called me, I immediately called and emailed everyone I knew to get prayers going. Within hours, prayer chains were picking up on our need, and thousands of people were praying for the little boy.

That morning, they performed surgery on the baby to get tubes into his lungs to help him breathe. The parents were not even allowed to touch him, and were told that they should probably get prepared for his death. They gave them no hope for recovery.

God wasn't done yet though.

The next day Trevor made a 100% improvement. Amazed, the doctors began to take him off oxygen, and eventually, their tests revealed that there was no brain damage. A week later, Trevor went home.

The hospital began to call him a "miracle baby." He had 11 things wrong with him, and the doctors said he was the most critical baby they had in their hospital for several years, but a week later, nothing was wrong with him.

—Patricia Rutherford

The Flagman

I was really looking forward to a weekend away with my family. As soon as I got off work on Friday, my wife and my 4-year old daughter started our six hour drive to our getaway retreat.

I had underestimated just how much time I needed this weekend, and found that I really was having a hard time driving. Halfway through the trip my daughter and wife were sleeping soundly, and I was fighting fatigue.

With an hour left to go, I was really having a hard time keeping alert. I knew I shouldn't be driving, but figured we were nearly there, so I continued. Then, my eyes locked on a construction flagman in the middle of the road waving for me to turn left. My reaction time was not what it should have been but, I turned just in time to make the detour.

My heart was pounding like crazy. Fully awakened by my near miss, I stopped the car to calm down and got out to see what kind of construction would be going on so late at night.

I was surprised to see no construction and no flagman.

I walked over to see that the road had ended there, and not far beyond that was a cliff that we most certainly would have flown over had we not turned when we did.

—Ron Williams

Angel on Ice

It was a winter day in the small town where my 2 1/2-year-old daughter Jennifer and I lived. The streets were very icy, and as much as I would have preferred to stay safely inside, we did have business to take care of that I just couldn't put off.

With Jennifer's car seat up in the front with me, we negotiated our way through the slippery roads without any problem. As it got near lunch time, I decided to pull into an alley next to where a friend of mine worked to see if we could eat together.

The alley was covered in ice. I slowly moved, skidding occasionally but making progress to the side door. When I got there, I stopped the car, but left it running long enough to run to the door and ask my friend what she was in the mood to eat. The sound of the car going into gear caught my attention. I watched as the car began moving in reverse. Jennifer had managed to kick the gear shift, and the car was moving backward through the icy alley, toward a busy street full of oncoming traffic.

I ran along side the car trying to open the door, but the car wasn't going straight because of the ice so I ended up under the back drivers' side of the car, my leg was twisted behind me and I was smashed up against the wall. Being against the wall the car had slowed down, but it was still was moving and I was being dragged along, helpless to do anything about it.

Then, out of nowhere, a woman walked up and calmly asked my daughter to unlock the door. She then got in, put it in park, and shut off the engine. Her complete composure was what sticks in my mind to this day. She wasn't the least bit rushed, nervous, or excited as you would expect someone to be in this circumstance. She then came around the car, pushed the car away from me, handed me my keys and gave me a hug. I got up, more shaken than injured, checked my daughter and then turned to thank the woman.

She was gone.

—Sheri Slover

Rockslide

*T*his actually happened to some friends of mine as they were driving down an isolated mountain road.

"As we went through the winding pass, we saw rocks tumbling down the mountainside in front of us. At first they were the size of baseballs but bigger ones began tumbling across the road as we got closer. I stopped the car, wondering if we could get around all the rocks in the road when I looked out my window to see these large boulders rolling toward the car!

"I could tell that these boulders would easily roll over the car, and as they picked up speed I knew it was all over. It was clear that at the rate they were coming, I wasn't going to be able to get away in time.

"We braced ourselves for the worst, waiting to get crushed by the oncoming rocks when, to our amazement, they all stopped at the edge of the road, several feet from the car. There was no reason for them to stop.

"They were tumbling with such force that they should have continued right over us and on down the rest of the mountain, yet, they stopped."

Before my friends turned the car around to go back the way they came, they took a picture of giant boulders to show their friends.

When they developed the picture they were surprised to see a figure of a man standing right by the rocks with his hand on them, as if holding them back.

They knew that nobody was standing there when they took the picture, and are convinced to this day, that this was their Guardian Angel.

—Jill Ming

Expected to Die

*A*t 26 years old, with two small children, I didn't have time for sickness and tragedy. I had been married for eight years and life seemed to be happening in the way it was supposed to, with PTA meetings, church functions and the usual happenings that punctuate people's lives.

Then I got sick. The pain was chronic, and I began to walk with a limp. The condition continued to progress to the point where I was actually crippled. It became a fight just to breathe, and even that struggle alone was enough to leave me without energy.

My husband was trying to go to school and work and he had to help me and take care of us all. It was a very difficult time for us. And it became even more difficult when the doctor told me to get my affairs in order because, at age 28, I was going to die within the year.

My husband and I believed in God, and went to church, but didn't fully comprehend what it meant to really give your life to Christ. That is until we met Brother Joe.

My husband is a film collector and was asked by a little Baptist church to show the film, "Life of Christ." While he was there, he met Brother Joe who ministered to him, listened to him, prayed with him and led him to a saving relationship with the Lord. After that, he invited my husband and I to come to the service the following Sunday, encouraging us, in light of my health problems, to go to the altar for prayer.

When we walked in that day, he motioned for us to sit with him. They were singing "I Surrender All." Something moved in my heart and the tears started to flow.

All to Jesus I surrender, all to Him I freely give
I will ever love and trust Him,
In His presence daily live.

I had never heard the song before in my church, but I was singing the words. I raised my hands, which was something we also never did at my church, and sang the song as a prayer to God.

I surrender all, I surrender all,
All to Thee my precious Savior,
I surrender all

As I sang out, I felt a hand reach inside of me, I know how it must sound, but I felt it move into my body and then felt a jerk as the sickness inside of me was ripped out. As this sensation occurred I heard a sound, similar to the sound contact paper makes when it's pulled apart.

All to Thee my precious Savior,
I surrender all

I knew right then that I was healed.

I began to scream and cry. My husband thought I was losing it and took me away, making up his mind that we wouldn't be going back to that church again. It wasn't until later when I explained what happened and when the hospital confirmed that I was healed that the full meaning of what happened that day became clear.

MIRACLES

At Columbia Hospital my healing is recorded! The doctor, after treating me for the flu two months later, said. "Well, we either treated you wrong for two years or you got a miracle!"

We got a Miracle! Praise the Lord

—*Rev. Carolyn Madden*

Carolyn and Howard were both ordained ministers in 1994 and are the founders of SEED Ministries, an outreach aimed at the inner cities, and other places and situations that are hostile toward the gospel.

Snowlight

*A*few years ago, my husband was diagnosed with choriocarcinoma, a type of testicular cancer. He was only 23 as he began numerous cancer treatments. At one point during his treatment, he began to bleed internally, resulting in emergency exploratory surgery. They almost lost him then but got him stable in time to find a tumor the size of a football that had caused the hemorrhage.

Another surgery was planned for two days later. Things looked grim though, and the doctors prepared me for the worst.

I stayed with him every minute, holding his hand and praying. We kept the television on as the hours went by, but didn't really watch it until a show about angels came on.

It was one of those reenactment shows, where they told one story after another of healings, miracles and visits by angels. In one segment, a man was praying for his son to be healed, and it happened.

Inspired, I asked my husband if he would let me pray to God to heal him. He couldn't talk because he had a breathing tube in his mouth, but he nodded his head, "Yes".

I began to pray.

I asked God to please, send angels, and to touch my husband and make him well. I just kept saying the same prayer over and over.

As I prayed, I looked up and saw what looked like snow made of light falling on my husband. It was like out of a movie. He didn't appear to see it, so I didn't mention it to him at the time—figuring maybe it was a figment of my imagination. Still though, deep down, I felt that in that very moment, God had heard me and intervened.

Later, while in the ICU room with my husband, his father called from Massachusetts to tell us about a woman from church who had seen a vision about his son. She said she had seen him in ICU with angels surrounding his bed.

I brought up what I had seen while I was in the ICU room praying. I looked over at my husband and as I described the snow made of light, my husband began to nod. I asked him if he saw it too. He nodded his head, "Yes!".

So much for my overactive imagination. We all praised God, knowing then and there all would be well.

As for my husband, he made it through just fine. Two years have passed and as far as his cancer goes, the last time he had a check-up, he was normal.

—*Sherry Cominos*

Motorcycle Miracle

*I*had been riding motorcycles for 24 years and consider myself an experienced rider. Avoiding major accidents and having close calls have always been part of the program, but well worth the freedom that comes with having two wheels on the ground and the open road ahead.

On Memorial Day, I was riding my motorcycle on a divided two-lane highway. I was less than a mile from my house and going a little faster than I should have been as it was familiar territory. How I missed seeing it, I still don't know, but a black truck suddenly pulled out in front of me. I was going too fast to stop, and there was no way around him.

I was going through it.

I only had time to think to myself, *this is it, my life about to end. I am going to die and there is no way out.* I grit my teeth, tightened my body and plowed into the truck.

I had expected everything to just go dark as I had been knocked out in another incident a few years earlier. This time, however, I was fully aware and expecting to get catapulted over the truck into oncoming traffic. Much to my surprise though, after hitting the truck, instead of going forward as every law of physics would predict, I felt myself flying backward in the air landing on the pavement away from all the traffic. Even the police report said that I must have been travelling from the other direction to wind up where I did. But, as I never lost consciousness, I knew the truth.

I didn't get off scot free. My leg and my wrist were both injured, but at the speed I hit that truck at, I should have been nothing more than a memory.

—John Wiley Stuff

Saved from Drowning

When I was 12, I was in a swimming pool aboard a large ship returning to the United States from Germany. My Dad was in the military, and we traveled quite a bit. I had a friend with me in this indoor pool, and we were the only two in the water at the time.

I could not swim, but my friend had convinced me I could hold onto the edge of the pool while she swam. I agreed to join her and was having lots of fun. Her brother hollered at her to come get ready for dinner, so she got out and went to her cabin, leaving me alone in the water.

Common sense told me I should not be alone, but I had gotten so relaxed and comfortable I decided to stay in for a while longer.

My hands lost their hold on the side of the pool, and I had somehow gotten in an area of water way over my head. So I began to panic, sinking under the water and rising back up. Each time I surfaced I tried to scream for help but water flooded into my mouth and I swallowed it in. I did this three times, getting heavier and heavier until I no longer rose to the surface. I realized I was going to drown. In that moment I thought of my Mom and Dad, my sister and brothers, how sad they would be when told that I had drowned. My heart ached for the pain my death would cause them. I closed my eyes as my lungs were bursting for air and I was going to have to give in and breathe in the water. My final thought was "God help me!"

I felt a pressure from behind me (like powerful giant arms) lifting my body from the water. One moment I was drowning and the next I was standing bewildered at the shallow end of the pool. I immediately turned around to embrace the huge person who had lifted me, but there was nobody there! I knew instantly that my guardian angel had saved me. There was no other explanation. My final little prayer to God had been heard.

—*Sylvia Maddux*

Caller I.D.

When I was in the scouts, I was required to sleep in the woods by myself. I was actually fine with the idea of having an adventure, but my mother and grandmother were both really worried for me.

Being a religious lady, my grandmother decided to pray for me and called a friend of hers that she often prayed with. When her friend didn't pick up, my grandmother decided not to bother her with a message and just hung up the phone.

It turned out that her friend had Caller ID, and when she got home, she recognized my grandmother's number. It was far too late to call, but knowing it was probably for a prayer request, she prayed anyway, without knowing the specific needs, or even who she was praying for.

Meanwhile, I was out in the woods, settling in for the night. While I wasn't scared about this during the days leading up to it, being alone in the dark wilderness was a little frightening after all. As I sat there, wondering what might be lurking in the shadows, I saw a small green light come up slowly over the woods. Eventually, it ended up hovering in the sky over my camp site—illuminating everything in a soft warm glow. I couldn't tell where it originated, and didn't really want to go out exploring for an answer, but it had a calming effect on me. I went to sleep without fear, as it glowed steadily until morning.

When I returned home, I told my grandmother what happened and discovered that when her friend got the call for an unknown prayer request, she prayed these words;

"Let the light of God shine on him."

—*Stan S.*

A Glimpse of Heaven

My mother was dying. She had been bedridden for the past four years and knew it was coming. One day though, she seemed especially at peace with the idea, almost as if she were looking forward to it.

When I asked why, she said that she had an experience which she related to me.

She said her room filled with glowing, winged beings. They smiled warmly and softly touched her skin, beckoning her to follow them. They lifted her up and in a short time, she found herself walking in a beautiful garden. There were flowers, fountains and more angels around. She said the whole place glowed, but not with sunlight. She compared the difference between that light and the sun's was like the difference between overhead lighting and a flashlight.

She had not been able to walk for so long that being able to do it then was an incredible feeling. She felt alive again.

The angels flew about her and lifted her up again. She said they were so gentle and tender with her, and that their eyes were filled with love. Their wings felt like silk and shimmered like satin. They spoke in whispers and encouraged her to wait for their soon return.

Smiling, Mom said that no one should ever be afraid to die. That we really do go to a beautiful place when we leave our bodies behind.

She died six weeks later, and I don't believe she even looked back.

Her courage in the face of certain death gives me the courage to face an uncertain life.

—*Dorothy Womack*

Warm and Safe

I was in a head-on car accident. I remember people yelling over me and talking about "cutting her clothes off." I saw something light and felt something warm and knew it was okay to let go.

Nobody spoke to me or anything like that. I just knew I didn't have to hold on as hard as I was trying.

I was in a coma for two weeks and I felt warm and safe there. The feeling of security was like something I had never known. I felt absolutely at peace and completely content in this place between places.

Then, that same light told me it was time to go back. I don't have any proof that it was an angel, but it is something I just know.

Why I was in that place of peace and didn't just go on to eternity, I don't know. Maybe I was spared some pain there, or maybe I was just given a place to rest my soul.

Regardless, I came back knowing that while life is a gift that should be treasured, what is beyond is safe and warm.

—Anne Talley

Miracle on Route 348

*I*t was a warm summer night and my wife, myself and two children were at my sister-in-law's house in Reading, Pa. When we left for home, it was approximately 8:30 P.M. Having a two hour ride ahead, I decided that I was too tired to drive, so my wife, Susan, took the wheel. After a short time, our two children, Jennifer and Amanda, and I fell into a deep sleep. I remember waking up when we were about 30 minutes from home. We were driving through a construction site and Susan was very tired. I offered to take the wheel but Susan decided that she could drive the rest of the way with no problem, so I went back to sleep. The rest of my memories of that trip and night are like snapshots that I will never forget!

When we were three miles from our house, Susan fell asleep behind the wheel. I really don't know what happened to the car. The first snapshot that I remember is waking up and telling Jennifer and Amanda that we had been in an accident and checking them to make sure they were all right. I then proceeded to force my door open to get out of the car. I know from the damage that was done that the car must have rolled over and smashed into a deep ditch on the shoulder of the road, causing the car to literally stand on end and then come to rest on its wheels.

The next snapshot is horrifying to say the least and something that I will never forget. Upon exiting the car I looked towards the driver's side as I heard my wife screaming that she had no control of her head. I saw her holding her head between her hands so she could look at me, and have some control of her head. I have never seen a look of horror and pain in anyone's eyes like I saw in the eyes of the woman I so love.

The next thing I remember is someone sitting her in a lawn chair and then getting into the ambulance. The rest of the accident scene is just a horrifying blur that I have no recollection of.

When we arrived at the hospital, we were put into different exam rooms. After I was checked out and found to be in good shape, except for some cuts and bruises, my father-in-law entered the room. It was then that I learned that Susan had broken her neck as well as a number of ribs. The break in her neck was a bad one and was very high up. If her spinal cord had been severed she would most likely have died as she would not be able to breathe on her own. At best, if the ambulance had arrived soon enough to save her she would be on a respirator and in a wheelchair, paralyzed from the neck down, for the rest of her life!

I remember laying there and waiting for the doctor to come in and the fear that gripped me. I remember praying and being impatient, as I just wanted to see my wife and assure her that everything would be all right, I knew that God was in control.

Finally the neurosurgeon came in and told me what had happened, it was then that both he and I realized the magnitude of the miracle that had taken place. He explained the broken vertebrae was pressing on Susan's spinal cord. He also told me that if she had moved after the accident or the paramedics had not immobilized her head properly, she would have been paralyzed from the head down for the rest of her life. I explained to the doctor that she had gotten out of the car and was walking around holding her head up with her hands. The doctor said it was a miracle that her spinal cord was not severed or at best that she had some form of paralysis. Even then though, with an operation likely, we were still not out of the woods.

After our talk, I was allowed to go to my wife's room. Here, laying on a rack was the woman that I loved; lying there with a device bolted into her skull so traction could be used to keep her neck straight and immobilized. I fought back tears, not wanting to alarm her. She was conscious and concerned about the children and me. I assured her that everyone was all right.

The next day when the neurosurgeon came in to examine Susan, he indicated that surgery was needed to put the broken vertebrae in place and relieve the pressure on the spinal cord. This was a very serious operation and it appeared as if it would most likely result in Susan having paralysis of some sort. He said that he would operate the next day, as soon as Susan was stabilized.

I can't explain the peace that I felt, even after hearing the news that surgery was needed. I was praying as well as our church and a number of churches in the area. You see we serve a God that is in control and I prefer to believe the report of the Lord, not the report of man. I knew that everything would be all right, that the Lord was in control.

When the doctor came in the next morning, he said he had been reviewing the case and decided that he would not operate! Praise the Lord! He said that he felt that a halo brace could be used and the bone would slip into place when the brace was put on.

Susan was measured for the brace and in two days, it was ready to be put on. The procedure took a lot less time than the neurosurgeon anticipated and praise the Lord; the bone went into place perfectly. Approximately 10 days later Susan was free to go home.

When we went to the neurosurgeon for Susan to have a check-up a few weeks later we were stunned at what we learned.

The doctor showed us the x-rays of Susan's neck. Her spinal cord was in the shape of a rough S from the vertebrae pressing on it. It was incredible to see how far it had been pushed down and not severed.

Images flooded my mind of the day this happened, when she held her head in her hands, a fraction of an inch from death. The doctor said that he had never seen a case such as this one, where the patient had no ill affects when so much pressure was on the spinal cord.

Today, Susan leads an active life with no pain, or symptoms of any kind. She loves to do aerobics, walk, play tennis and go bowling. I am truly a rich and blessed man and many times, I just stand in awe, when I think of the miracle that I am married to. I know that true wealth lies in the love that we have for one another and the good health that we take for granted. I thank the Lord for everything that He has done; He truly is the great physician.

— *Sam Balducci*

Tail Wind

*I*t was a warm September day and some friends and I decided to hurl ourselves from an airplane at 6,000 feet. This was actually my 30th-birthday present. We arrived and signed up for a class that would prepare us for what we were about to face. The class was designed to familiarize us with the equipment, how to operate it, and how to handle any situation that may come up. The class lasted for five hours and we were quizzed over and over and made to act and react out safety techniques.

Finally, it was my turn to go up for my first jump with one of my friends. With the training fresh in our heads, we still remembered that once we left the plane we were on our own. We chose to do an instructor-assisted deployment. This means that the instructor pulls the pilot chute (a small parachute that is released and fills with air to pull the main parachute from the backpack) and throws it as the jumper leaves the plane. Once out of the plane, the rest is up to the jumper. A few minutes before our jump, they switched the type of plane we would jump from—this meant the training of leaving the plane we had in the morning no longer applied. They gave us a quick run-through of how to leave the new plane and a few minutes later we were airborne.

I was the first jumper. We climbed to 6,000 feet, and I spotted my target. My jumpmaster pulled my pilot chute and I positioned myself to exit the plane. He gave me the signal and I went. I counted to six (like instructed) and looked up over my left shoulder to see that my parachute had not opened fully or correctly. I was falling like a rock. I identified the malfunction and thought I was to blame. I performed the corrective measures just as I was taught. At first it seemed to work, but it didn't! I checked my altimeter and I was at 3500 feet. The panic point is 2000 feet—this is where (no matter what) you release (pull the cut-away cable) the main parachute and immediately deploy the reserve parachute.

I decided that the error had to be mine so I tried once more to get my main parachute to open. To be honest, I was not scared. I was too busy trying to figure a way out of the situation and I was asking God for help. Though I tried the corrective measures once more, the main parachute failed to open. I checked my altimeter again and I was at 1900 feet. I responded immediately by pulling the cut-away cable for the main parachute and immediately deployed my reserve parachute. I thanked God out loud! I, then, had to assess where I was because I had fallen far from my scheduled mark.

The helmet I was wearing was equipped with a one-way radio (I could receive only.) But I was too far from the airport to hear the spotter's (the jumpmaster on the ground watching my jump) instructions. Now my concern was landing safely...I did as I was taught. I could no longer see the airport where I was to land so I picked a Soft Open Flat Area (called a SOFA) and was headed toward it when I heard the first crack of my radio, "If you can hear me, make a hard left turn." I immediately made the turn showing the spotter that I could now hear him. "You're pretty low and pretty far from the airport but we're going to try to get you back over here." I kept the parachute as true to the course as I could. Each time you turn a parachute you lose a lot of altitude. Finally I could see it...but I was only at 400 feet and falling fast. I knew there were power lines between the airport and me.

To have survived the parachute malfunction and then wind up on power lines made it seem inevitable that someone upstairs was out to get me. But then, scant feet away from electrocution, a tail wind came from behind, lifting me over the power lines letting me down at the airport. Safe at last.

Of the 200-300 persons at the airfield that day, every eye was on me. Everyone knew I was a student and this was my very first jump and when I touched down I was enveloped in a mass of people congratulating me. People of all jumping experiences wanted to know what it was like and how I did it. It was simple—I did what I had to do—the rest was faith.

Later, while talking to my spotter, I learned that he was telling me on the radio to cut away the main parachute as soon as I left the plane. He could see right away that my parachute had a "non-recoverable" malfunction due to a packing error. I also learned that since I was not responding to his radio message (because I could not hear him) they had already called for an ambulance before I had opened my reserve parachute.

I have jumped 20 times since then, but I will never forget the lesson meant only for me that day. There is no longer fear when I plunge myself from an airplane. I learned that God's hand is in everything—sometimes it's a word, a smile, a thought and sometimes it's the breath of a tail wind in the just the right moment.

—*Keith Jones*

The Miracle of Forgiveness

*I*t was a typical Sunday evening when my husband Terry, Breanna our daughter, and I stopped by the small store my mother-in-law ran. We usually stopped there on our way to church, to hang out while Grandma Brenda gave Breanna candy.

I usually stand behind the counter with Brenda while Breanna sits next to me on the floor.

A well-dressed man came in, got himself a drink and was paying for gas. As Brenda opened the register, he pulled out a gun and showed it to Terry, telling him to get behind the counter.

Terry reached down and scooped up Breanna, wanting to protect her, but the man put the gun within an inch of her head.

Although I should have been terrified by the unfolding events, I felt a strange peace, and new that God was with me at that very moment. I prayed, "Lord Jesus, protect us."

I didn't know if we would live or not, but I knew I was not afraid. I looked at the man in the face.

As he wasn't wearing a mask, I thought for sure he would kill us to prevent himself from being identified. Terry and Brenda begged for the gunman to spare Breanna's life.

"Please don't hurt her... she's just a baby!"

Rather than talk to him though, I chose to continue talking to the Lord. Jesus had never failed me before, and somehow I knew then that he was watching out for us now.

The man took the money and left the store.

I took Breanna and fell to my knees. All I could do was thank God for protecting her. Brenda was already on the phone with 911. Within five minutes, the man was apprehended by the police.

You would think the story would stop here with a happily ever after, but there was more to come.

As we waited to identify the man at the police station, I felt my anger grow with every passing second.

How dare he put my baby's life in danger!

I went to the restroom to compose myself. It was there that the Lord impressed upon me a simple message. "Sherry, you have to forgive him, I love him too."

I knew what was right. I knew God was right. I had to forgive him.

We did identify him and he was placed under a $1 million bond. From that day on, I began to pray for him. I prayed for months until the day he was sentenced. That day in the courtroom, something happened.

He pled guilty, knowing he was going to go to prison for 30 years. Then he turned to us and told us that he was sorry for what he had done, and that he had made Jesus, the Lord of his life.

At that moment, I no longer saw the man who was holding a gun to my child's head. I saw myself standing before God saying, "Please forgive me." It was then that I truly forgave him, remembering that Jesus didn't think twice before he forgave me.

So, for anyone who reads this, receive this. It doesn't matter what you have done. Jesus will forgive you. And if someone has hurt you and you think you can't forgive, remember how God forgave you. He loves everyone, even that person you think is unloveable.

—Sherry Kindley

The Wrong Turn

I was driving home from the store with my son, going a different route than I had ever gone before. I didn't really know why I felt compelled to make the turns that I did, but I went with it, enjoying the company of my boy.

As we drove though, our conversation came to a halt as I saw a child laying in the middle of the street, obviously the victim of a hit and run.

I pulled over, running to him as fast as I could, and did the first thing that came to mind. I laid hands on him and started praying. I felt angels all around him and knew Jesus was with him, and he wanted me to keep praying.

My boy ran to a nearby house and got help. In moments, an ambulance arrived, taking the boy away.

The next day, I went to the hospital. His father told me he had bleeding on the brain, so I asked him if I could pray for him again. He agreed, so I laid hands on his head, prayed and knew he was healed. The next day he was up walking around. Jesus healed him.

I know now that the Lord lead me down that road because I never drive that way home. It was a miracle of God! Amen!

—Anonymous

Dream Angel

*E*ven though it happened in a dream I have always felt that an angel did something wonderful for me. My 12-year-old Grandson had died suddenly in an accident. The grief was unbearable. The scene that played over and over in my mind was the very last time I saw him. His 14-year-old sister had spent the night with me and I took her home and was backing out of the driveway when I saw my grandson in their yard and we waved and smiled at each other. Of course I didn't know I would never see him again or I would have taken the time to give him a big hug.

Three days later he was gone. After several weeks of agonizing grief I dreamed about an angel bringing him down from heaven in her arms. It was an awesome scene. I can't possibly describe it. We gave each other a wonderful hug and just as suddenly as the angel came down it returned to the heavens with my grandson. I know it was a dream, but it helped me through my grief more than any other thing. It was the most realistic dream I have ever had. Even though it has now been 14 years the dream is still very vivid in my mind.

God has used dreams in the past, and this time, he made one just for me.

Thank you, God.

—Lorrene Lemaster

A believer sees more on his knees than a philosopher sees on his tiptoes.

In the Presence of The King

O n Ash Wednesday, we had an evening church service. I had
been looking forward to it all day and very much enjoyed
being there. When it came to an end, Brother Randy asked us to come
forward as we felt the Spirit call us and pray at the altar. He then
anointed our forehead with a cross out of ashes.

Not one to let anything stand between God and myself, I went to
the altar and knelt down to pray. There was a peace there for me and
an overwhelming sense that I was in a Holy Place.

As I was awaiting my cross to be placed on my forehead, with my head bowed I opened my eyes, I realized I did not see Randy but rather saw Jesus Christ.

I looked up in awe as I saw Him standing before me. Then I closed my eyes and received my cross on my forehead. When I opened them again, I saw an angel appear. The angel had on a white robe and wings and was in female form. It was as if I could reach out and touch her. I knew I was in the presence of our Lord and Savior Jesus Christ and His angels.

This renewed my faith to say the least, for God has truly touched me.

—Alex Kiss

Never Alone

*I*t was finally summer, and my friend Amy and I decided to go on our first vacation as "adults." I had just completed my first year of college while Amy had just completed her second. We packed up my car and set off to Dallas, Texas.

Amy was driving at a speed of around 70 mph when the car started to rock like crazy. Something was terribly wrong. The car spun out of control and landed in the large median facing the lane we had just been traveling in.

When we came to rest, I couldn't open my door, so I crawled out the window. Afraid the car would catch fire, Amy tried desperately to open her door. She was trying with all her might but with no luck.

I told her to climb out the window, but she was paralyzed with fear.

Right then a giant of a man came over smiling. He walked over to her door and opened it as easily as if there was nothing wrong with it.

"God was with you", he said.

Amy got out and we hugged each other as the police got to the scene. Other witnesses stopped and gave statements to the police, but the nice man who let her out of the car was nowhere to be found.

It turned out that our rear axle had snapped. The police officer said that he had never seen anyone survive an accident like ours before. He told us at that high of a speed, we should have been dead.

The officer was right. We should have died, but didn't because God and one of His Angels, was with us.

—Steffanie Flack

Rearview Mirror

One morning as I was out running errands, I noticed people were driving a bit more aggressively that usual. It was getting so bad that I was actually thinking of just putting off what I needed to do until another day. Duty won out however, and I continued on my way.

As I pulled out of the driveway toward my next stop, a car came out of nowhere, heading straight for me. I was only in first gear and was going slow to get out of the way. I tried to move, but he was coming too fast. On my right there was a ditch and on my left there was traffic. With nowhere to go, I grabbed the steering wheel and braced myself for the worst. Our eyes met and his mirrored the terror that filled mine. I turned my head, closed my eyes and prayed three words.

"Jesus, Jesus, Jesus..."

One second went by, followed by another and then another.
Nothing happened.
No impact—no sound of squealing tires—nothing.
I looked up to find that he was gone and nowhere in sight. The car that was on a collision course to hit me, had vanished.
All I could do was thank Jesus.

—*Dorinda Kay Williams*

"The Scripture says there is a time to be born and a time to die. And when my time to die comes, an angel will be there to comfort me. He will give me peace and joy even at that most critical hour, and usher me into the presence of God, and I will dwell with the Lord forever. Thank God for the ministry of His blessed angels."

—Billy Graham

Hush, my dear, lie still and slumber!
Holy angels guard thy bed!
Heavenly blessings without number
Gently falling on thy head.

—A Cradle Hymn
Isaac Watts 1674-1748

The Faithful Heart

When I was a little, I was playing outside with a neighbor boy much older than me. As we jumped off the swing to play in the sandbox he became enraged about something and hit me in the temple with a wooden croquet mallet. I was rendered unconscious by the blow. My mother and uncle rushed me down the block to the doctor's house where an ambulance happened to be waiting. I started to go into convulsions one after another and the doctor feared the worst.

They got me to the hospital, and although it appeared as if I would die that night, I did pull through. Although I did live, my troubles were far from over as I continued with what is called severe grand mal seizures. I also had to wear thick glasses because my eye muscles were damaged. I was constantly in the hospital all alone and very scared.

Any time I could find a preacher or a priest to come to my room, I would have them read from the Bible to me and get them to say prayers with me for all the kids. I was at the hospital so much that I felt like I worked there and would make rounds to the other patients to try and get them to smile.

I was always being heavily medicated because they could not control the seizures and felt I would not live very long if this continued. I would have one seizure after another followed by severe headaches and loss of balance.

God told me in a dream though, that I had to be prayed for three times, then touched by God and then I would receive my healing.

After getting three people to pray for me, I was getting ready for bed when something unforgettable and strange happened. I know it will sound weird, but this did happen.

As I walked into the bedroom I saw a man standing at the end of the bed. I knew then he was not good. Deep inside my spirit, I knew he was the devil himself, but what did he want? I was scared and even screamed for several minutes, but no one heard me. Then, instead of running, I walked toward him yelling for Jesus and climbed into bed.

I begged for Jesus to hold my hand. At the name of Jesus, the devil disappeared. The next morning when I awoke, my grandma told me my hand was in the air all night and she could not put it down, as if someone were holding it. It did not drop to my side until I awoke in the morning. Not only did God touch me, but he held my hand all night!

After that, I quit having seizures. And a year later I stopped wearing glasses. This miracle was from God.

—*Michele C.*

It's Okay

his all happened when I was about seven years old, yet it is as vivid a memory as if it happened just yesterday.

It happened right after my parents had divorced. My mom and I were staying at a friend's house. My mom was asleep and so was her friend. For some reason I had chosen to sleep on the floor in the living room.

That night I stayed up thinking about my parents and thinking maybe they broke up because of me. I was full of despair, and I felt completely alone. I began to cry.

Then the room began to get filled with a soft light which got progressively brighter with every second. The light was so bright that I was sure my mom would wake up.

Then, from the center of all the brightness, a figure emerged dressed like you would picture Jesus dressing.

"It is okay." the figure said.

It wasn't like words you hear with your ears, but words you hear with your whole body, mind and soul. He was telling me that none of this was my fault and that I am never alone.

I wasn't the least bit afraid. I felt this wave of inner peace go through me and felt calm and relaxed. I fell asleep with a knowledge that God really does love and care for each of us.

—Annabelle P.

...lo, I am with you always, even to the end of the age. —Jesus Christ

The Lifeguard

When I was 10, my father took my brother and I to Galveston island. We had just finished eating, so we took off for the beach, forgetting to tell my father where we would be.

We got to the shoreline, and I dove into the water as my brother stopped to play in the sand. I began swimming out to a sand bar, but as I kept swimming, the current began to drag me further and further from the shore. When I realized that I could no longer touch the ocean floor, I began to panic. I screamed for my brother and began to thrash in the water wildly. My brother ran for the beach house where my parents were, but my energy was running out, and I began to sink below the surface.

As I did, I could see only brown water above me. After a few seconds however, I saw a man's face appear above me. He reached down into the water, and brought me to the surface. This man was very fit, and he had almost perfect features. He was completely quiet, and he made no facial expressions at all. He was almost non-human in a way. He brought me to where the water came up to my knees, and then he sat me down.

I leaned over to catch my breath, but when I stood up to thank him, he was gone. I walked the rest of the way to the shore and asked my brother if he had seen the man who had just saved my life.

He looked at me with a crazy expression, and said "What man, we are the only ones on this beach. There is no one else in the water."

As I looked around, I saw that this was true. We could see miles of shoreline, and no one else was near.

—Brian Allen

The Hands of an Angel

On a Friday evening in the summer, I was following behind friends who were driving a huge Lincoln Town car. I had a subcompact Plymouth Champ and could barely see around the Lincoln. Suddenly, the Lincoln swerved out into the left lane passing a Ford mini-truck which was sitting dead-still in the middle of the road trying to turn left into his driveway. I slammed on my brakes, tried to steer right but hit his bumper going about 45 mph!

Because seatbelt use was not a law then, I didn't have one on. But, as I slammed into the back of that truck, I felt powerful hands rest on my shoulders.

They held me in my seat. I did not hit the steering wheel, fly through the windshield or even move out of my seat!

MIRACLES

The wife of the man whose truck I hit, came running out of her house and over to my car. She helped me out and couldn't believe I was okay.

My car was totalled, and although I was terribly shaken, I was not hurt! I was sore for the next few days, but if it hadn't been for my guardian angel, I would surely have died.

—Anonymous

God, You Can Stop
The Car Now

*T*he weather was bad on the morning I was supposed to leave for my doctor's appointment, so bad, in fact, that my husband, Don, suggested that I leave a little earlier than usual. I took his advise, but wouldn't you know it, I had an accident anyway.

I was in the outside lane of five lanes, next to the median, and there was a shoulder on each side (making seven lanes, really). As I approached Atlanta, the traffic was heavy, but it was moving at 50 mph.

There was a two-car lead between me and the car up front, so I glanced down at the piece of paper I was holding in my hand, quickly, to double-check my exit number. When I looked back up, the car in front had stopped. I slammed on my brakes. My car did not stop—instead it went into a skid.

I directed the car to the shoulder on my left to keep from hitting the car in front. As I got up beside that car, my car jackknifed and went directly across the five lanes of traffic at 50 mph.

It felt as if someone had shot me from a slingshot across ice, the car was moving with so much force and speed.

There was a high embankment with a highway built over it, and I was headed straight for it. I actually thought that I might die in that crash. When my car hit the grassy ravine between the right-hand shoulder and the embankment, the car turned one complete revolution and I was facing the direction I had just come, but still traveling backwards at 50 mph.

I held on for dear life and was praying.

I couldn't see where I was headed—whether I would hit a car, or an embankment. The car started down a ravine. At that moment I prayed, "God, you can stop this car right now, in Jesus' Name." The car turned facing the embankment and stopped still, right side up, with the front tires on one side of a cement drain and the back tires on the other side.

I was shaking like a leaf. I had not hit a single car, and no car had hit me. Aside from the fact we had slid all over the place, my engine was running smoothly, all my gauges read normally, and I appeared to be fine.

"Thank you, Jesus!" Then I looked up the highway. Cars had stopped all along the shoulder. People were watching and waiting in case I needed help, I guess.

I thought for a second and decided to try to back the car up on the shoulder, so I put the gear in reverse and slowly backed. After I got parked on the shoulder, facing the direction I should go, the people who had stopped to see if I was all right were already on their way, as perplexed undoubtedly as I was, that I was driving away from the incident that should have killed me.

When I returned home, I told Don that God had performed a miracle for me and described it. He asked me about what time it had happened. When I told him it was about 9:15, he said he was praying at 9:00 for God to keep an angel with me on the trip.

—Anna Leavell

Pictures of Angels

*A*lmost as soon as I brought my baby girl home from the hospital, I began to notice these strange arcs of light in pictures we took of her. Not every picture would have them—maybe just one or two out of every other roll. They didn't always occur in the same place on the pictures either, eliminating a defect in the lens of the camera as a suspect. As time went on, I began looking for these arcs of light and I began to identify them as her angels.

Other people were not so convinced the lights represented angels and always kind of laughed it off but this never swayed my opinion.

When she was around six months old I found out my daughter had some neurological problems which were affecting her development.

She was was an extremely quiet baby (no babbling like most babies) her legs were not the same length and there was some talk about cerebral palsy. An MRI of her brain showed that indeed she had suffered a mini stroke at some point, probably in utero. I was devastated and cried out to God night after night to please show me how to help my baby.

The first thing I did was to start going to church. I didn't belong to a church at that time but felt that now was the time to make some changes.

Soon after joining our church, they had an all-night service scheduled. It was too cold outside for the baby, and I really didn't feel up to it, so I decided to go to bed instead. While laying there though, I felt an overwhelming urge to get up and go anyway. I got up, knowing God wanted me there for a reason.

When I arrived, there was a time of prayer and ultimately an altar call. I was tearing up as I made my way to the altar to ask God for a healing. It was a very moving experience for me and I left there knowing something in our life had changed.

This happened last March. By Mother's Day, we went back up to that altar, but this time without a request. Instead we brought a "thank you." My daughters symptoms had disappeared! Even her legs were now the same length. Her therapist was astounded and I was full of praise at how great our God is.

After that day, the lights stopped appearing in her photos. That is until last Christmas. I was shocked as I looked at the Christmas pictures to see five pictures of my daughter, each with wings in them.

In one, the wing has an aura of light around it, one is the wing in an upright position which looks exactly like a dove's wing—it even shows depth and contour. A few are of the wing in a downward position. This time I didn't have to convince anyone what the pictures were. Its truly incredible!

Why they showed up in the pictures? I don't know. But I do know that she is truly a blessed little girl whose trials helped her mommy see the spiritual light.

—Robyn Jeter

To see these pictures in color, go to our website at
www.angelseverywhere.faithweb.com.

Lead Foot

My brush with angels happened one afternoon as I was in my car stopped at a red light. There was one car in front of me. My mother was in the front passenger seat and my son was in the back.

The light turned green and the car in front of me went on his way but I was unable to move. My foot was on the brake and it seemed to weigh about 500 pounds. *I couldn't lift it.*

I turned to my mother and I could see her lips moving, but I couldn't hear her. What I did hear was a type of singing that I have never heard before or since. If I had to try to describe it I would say it was a soothing "aaahhh" sound in perfect harmony. This wasn't the usual three-or four-note harmonies that go together. This was more like a thousand different notes coming together to make one chord.

It was the most beautiful sound I have ever heard. It started softly, lasted about five seconds. As it faded away I felt the weight in my foot leave. When the sound was gone, I was able to raise my foot to put it on the gas pedal.

I was shook up from the experience and was taking a breath to tell my mother what had happened. As I moved forward to the intersection, a car coming from the left flew through his red light crossing only inches from the front of my car flying at least 50 mph.

I know I would have been killed if I had not had this experience.

I announced to my mother and son that there was an angel in our car. My son said "Where? Where?" I smiled and for the next mile or so I can remember saying thank you out loud and in my heart. For the beautiful song that held me motionless and safely out of harms way.

—Suzanne Hagan

But if these beings guard you, they do so because they have been summoned by your prayers.

—Saint Ambrose

Angels on the Night Shift

About three years ago I was working the overnight shift alone at a local convenience store. On this particular night we had received about eight inches of snow and it was still snowing pretty hard.

It seemed to be shaping into a long, boring night. By 2 A.M. I had only seen three customers and the '70s music on the store system was putting me to sleep.

I started to stare out of the store window when I saw a car go by and I got this weird sensation of danger. I looked at the car and I can't explain it, but there seemed to be a darkness around it. I started to panic slightly because I was in the middle of nowhere with no one around and with the snow still falling it would take the police a while to arrive.

I went to the office to call the store manager when I heard the door buzzer go off. I came to the counter. Then a masked man came running up to me with a gun pointed at me demanding money. I can't put into words how terrified I was. I could only see the gunman's eyes because he had on a black ski mask.

After I gave him the money, he ordered me to turn around. I turned slowly, never so afraid in my life. Right then I felt a presence standing so close to me that I thought the gunman had jumped the counter.

I could see the gunman though, reflected in a glass pane. He was still where he was with the counter still between us. Still though, behind me it felt as if someone were close to me. I then had a feeling like whoever this invisible someone was, had their arms around me, giving me a hug. I felt warmth and a sense of assurance.

I could see the gunman pointing the gun at the back of my head from the reflection of the store window against the night sky. Then I heard the click as the trigger was squeezed.

Nothing.

Again, a click. Then I heard the gunman say some obscenities as he turned and ran out the door.

I hit the store alarm then ran to lock the door and then waited nearly 30 minutes for the police.

Later that morning I saw the video of the robbery from the store tape and everyone agrees that it appears that the gunman was trying to shoot me in the back but his gun was jamming up. When I saw that—I was in shock and also glad to just be unharmed.

The next night I had to work again because no one could be found to replace me. (No kidding!) All night I was on edge and a complete basket case. I started to pray to God to protect me and to get me through the night unharmed.

During the night, a beautiful, older woman came into the store and I remember she had on a purple blouse and was dressed professionally.

She came to the counter and I could smell something like lilacs or fresh flowers coming from her. Something about her manner quickly put me at ease as we chatted for a few minutes. She then turned to leave, but said one more thing.

"Don't worry, there are two seven-foot angels standing on either side of the doors." She smiled at me then walked out into the parking lot. I then noticed that she wasn't driving a car and I thought it seemed weird that an older woman would be walking to a convenience store by herself at about 1 A.M. and dressed like she was. I had no other customers so I walked out into the parking lot and I looked around but she was gone.

I left that job right afterward. After all, I didn't want my body guards to have to keep working overtime either!

—Name withheld on request

Spiderman

A VW for only $200! Too good of a deal to be true! I was stationed in San Diego and needed a car, so this came along at just the right price and at just the time. The fact it needed some work and a really good cleaning was to be expected. Lurking where I didn't see them, however, was something I didn't expect—a black widow's nest, alive with baby spiders.

As I was cleaning underneath the spare tire I came across the web. The babies were so small I didn't even see them, but was immediately attacked and severely bitten hundreds of times before I even knew what was happening.

MIRACLES

I was admitted into Balboa Naval Hospital intensive care ward. I had a welted ring of bites around my neck and numerous bites on my back. When the spiders are small, they are fuzzy and can flatten out and migrate on wind drifts which accounted for how I had been covered with them.

My condition was deteriorating quickly, as my body reacted to the venom. I was experiencing respiratory failure, and had blood clots forming. My lungs collapsed and I had a pulmonary hemorrhage with an enlarged heart. My own immune system began to attack everything made of protein which made my system begin to dissolve itself. My intestines were almost eaten right through, according to the colonoscopy, this caused gastro-intestinal hemorrhage, kidney failure, severe liver damage, and nerve damage. My doctors basically had given up on me and the report that was given to my commanding officer said they expected me to be dead by morning. A casualty report was even filled out with everything but the time of death.

It's funny what happens when you get that close to dying. As death approaches, it's important to get rid of baggage so you can travel light. Anger, hatred and bitter feelings weigh the most, so you begin to forgive and let them go. I forgave my ex-wife, and felt relief of another kind as I let everyone off the hook for any wrongs they had done to me. This must have pleased God, because I fell asleep and woke up in the morning smiling and feeling good.

The doctors were actually surprised to see that I had made it. It turned out that one of them expected me to be dead within eight minutes after he examining me, but here I was, the next day, smiling in bed.

Still, I was not out of the woods.

I was in my own room in the hospital and sound asleep the next night. It was about 4:50 A.M. I was on my right side and felt someone squeeze my left calf and with an urgent whisper say "THOMAS!" I looked over my left shoulder and to find no one there. I laid my head back down and about fell asleep when I felt the squeeze on my left calf again but harder and heard my name twice and more urgent saying "THOMAS! THOMAS!"

I spun my head and sat up to see that I was alone. I got up to look around the room and there, sitting in a chair to my left, was an angel.

The angel was physically shaped like a human but made of colored light. It sat there with legs crossed and arms on the rests, sitting up as if waiting for something to happen.

The RN on duty, Nurse Weaver, was doing her rounds and happened to be walking past my room and noticed I was standing. She immediately rushed in to see what was wrong, and as she came, the angel vanished. It turned out that I was in oxygen deprivation and heading toward respiratory failure. I was told that I would have probably passed away in my sleep had I not gotten the nurse's attention.

I have copies of Navy medical records to show how extremely bad my condition was. Doctors stated in the morning that it was nothing short of a miracle and people began calling me the "walking miracle". "I'm not, I just know who is!"

—*Thomas R Hanavan*

Thomas wishes to take this opportunity to thank God, the angel that woke him up, Samuel John Hanavan and Kenneth Copeland Ministries, The Bread of Life Church in Buffalo, N.Y., The Embassy Christian Center in Escondido, Ca,. Horizon Christian Fellowship of San Diego, Ca., Marin Christian Life Church in Ca. and the thousands of Christians from coast to coast and around the world that lifted him up in prayer when it went out by satellite.

Faith is the daring of the soul to go
farther than it can see.

The Shimmering

My daughter, Rachel, and I were at home alone in our house in Chandler, Arizona when we had our angelic experience.

We had been collecting angel things for years. There is something about the little statues and pictures that is comforting. At the same time, it keeps your mind wandering around the things of God which is always a good thing.

One day though, I was suffering through a real crisis of faith—knowing there was a God, but wondering at the same time. Then, this wave of peace flowed over me. There was this feeling of belonging and a sensation going through me that really I have no words to describe other than to say that for that moment, I was in the presence of unconditional love. I still don't know why, but I felt drawn to the kitchen.

There on the ceiling was a shimmering light. It looked like the sun shimmering off of water with all its little shimmers of light. At first the skeptic in me looked for a rational explanation but could find no source for the light. I thought I must be hallucinating or going crazy. I called out to my daughter to come downstairs. She came down and I asked her, "Rachel, do you see anything up there?"

"Mommy," she said, "that's an angel." We stood there together in awe of this beautiful angel for a few moments and then, of course, the skeptic in me again took control.

I went around the house and turned off all of the lights. My daughter helped me close all the shades. We cut off every source of light we could find until the house was dark, and then returned to the kitchen to find that our angel shimmered as brightly as before.

I finally gave in and fully accepted that we were seeing an angel. Rachel and I stood and talked to the angel for a little while. The angel never spoke back but when I spoke to it, the shimmers would change directions. It was so beautiful. The angel stayed for about 20 minutes after I was done trying to convince myself that it wasn't there. The whole thing swirled until it disappeared into the ceiling, leaving an image on our ceiling that didn't go away for days. It looked like it was a burn on our ceiling.

Since then, our lives have changed dramatically. I have become a Christian and have more faith than I ever have had. I was very unhealthy emotionally and physically and still have work to do, but I will never doubt again what I know to be true in the first place. I have faith in God and in myself and more love for God and my children and myself than I ever thought possible. And my daughter is attending church with me as well and she says that she will never forget our angel. For me, this angel saved my life and continues to do so. Anytime I feel my faith wavering or feel like I can't go on—I think of our angel and I'm reminded of how blessed Rachel and I were and are.

—Rachel Verich &
Michelle Edelstein

All I have seen teaches me to trust the creator
for all I have not seen.

—Ralph Waldo Emerson

The Invisible Wall

$\mathcal{A}$s a Pastor, I am often called into duty at odd hours. One night after 11:00 I got a call from a woman in Texas asking me to please check on her son. It seems that years before he wandered away from the Christian faith he'd been raised in. Now things weren't going well for him.

The mother continued to fill me in on the sad details. Earlier that evening, the son's wife had left him. The mother had been in phone contact with him a few hours before. He had been so despondent she feared he might commit suicide. Now his phone was off the hook. For all she knew, he might have hurt himself or be dying as we spoke.

I took the address, got dressed, and drove into town looking for an all-night filling station to get a map for the small city of where he lived. By the time I finally found a map, and located his address on it, it was well after 2:00 A.M.

Then I hit my next obstacle. He lived in a planned community where all the mailboxes were in front and none of the houses had numbers on them. On top of that, there were no streetlights either. There was no way I could match the mailbox with the house where the man lived. I couldn't simply go and get the police, either. (If his mom had wanted the police looking into this, she wouldn't have called me.) I didn't want to start his neighbors to gossiping and asking questions by knocking on doors at random. Yet I also couldn't go home and come back the next day. The man might have swallowed sleeping pills and be in need of medical attention for all I knew.

I had to find him now, I couldn't get human help, and I couldn't afford to knock on the wrong door at this time of the night. What was I going to do?

I parked my car at the foot of the road near the mailboxes and began walking up the unlit roadway. There were no lights, not even moon or stars. "God," I prayed, "I work for You. This is Your business, not mine. I've got to find the right house. Please help."

About 150-200 feet up the dark roadway between the silent houses, I ran into an invisible wall. I could see through it into the shadows of the roadway beyond. Yet I could put my hand on it. Immediately I knew I was getting the help I'd prayed for. I probably looked like one of those mimes you see on television feeling an invisible wall, except this was no act, and it was not make believe. It was as solid, rising straight and up crossing the pavement diagonally to my left. My fingers could press into the surface, perhaps a quarter of an inch—but it certainly wasn't going anywhere. It rose at least as high as my face.

I can only describe this wall as a powerful force field of some kind—but not electrical in nature. Something with more the solidness of gravity. With my right hand held up, I walked along its surface to the left, letting it guide me to the side of the road. The surface of this invisible barrier was seamless to my touch. I could see through it into the black-shadowed street beyond.

When I reached the edge of the road, I found a tall hedge, and in the hedge an opening with a gate. I would have passed it by in the darkness, not even knowing it was there. My pathway along the invisible wall had led me directly to it. I opened the gate, felt my way to the front door of the house and rang the bell. In a few minutes, a man opened the door. He was only wearing jeans. He still rubbed sleep from his eyes. Obviously, I had awakened him.

"I'm sorry to disturb you this late at night," I said, "but I'm looking for—" I gave the name of the man I was trying to find. The man stood for a moment, seemingly puzzled by my request. Then he said, "He doesn't live here, but his wife is in sleeping on our couch. Maybe you should talk to her." I talked with the woman for a few minutes, told her what had happened outside that helped me find her, and heard her side of the marital conflict. We had prayer together, and she told me where to find her husband. Their house was at the far end of the dark roadway up the hillside yet.

When I left the house where the wife was staying, the invisible wall that had led me to the gateway in the hedge was gone. The man I was all right. The phone had just slipped off the hook. I told him his mom just wanted me to check on him to be sure he was okay. Before I left, I also told him of the invisible wall, and how it had led me to find his wife a few minutes before. "God must have something good for both of you to give me this kind of help in finding you," I told him. Later, this couple came to church on several occasions and reconciled.

—*Pastor Skip Johnson*

Pastor Johnson can be reached at
skpNLJ@hotmail.com

Soldier Angel

*I*t was winter of 1952, I was home for the weekend from Vassar Brothers Hospital, Poughkeepsie, N.Y., where I was a student nurse.

I had to be back to school by 10:00 P.M. on Sunday. My family took me back to the train station in Fonda to catch the 6 o'clock train back to Poughkeepsie. We soon discovered the trains were all late due to storms in the area. It seemed like forever until they announced the train was coming. I boarded and found a seat by the window. I waved to mom and dad, and brother, Chuck—their faces appeared smaller and smaller as we pulled away from the platform.

Moments later, the conductor came by checking tickets. he looked at me and my ticket and said, "This train doesn't stop in Poughkeepsie, Miss, you're on the wrong train." Then he walked away. Here I was, an 18-year-old girl alone and wondering what to do. The conductor came back and told me this train would stop in Hudson, and I could get off there and wait for the right train. What a relief. My prayers had been answered. After an hour wait in Albany due to icy conditions, we were on our way again.

Arriving in Hudson at last, it was close to midnight, and I was past the 10 P.M. curfew. I entered the station and was shocked to see the big waiting room completely deserted. An odd feeling began to creep over me. I heard a noise in a back room and found a baggageman working there. He told me my train would be along in an hour. Here I was again, alone and afraid. I went into the waiting room, and I can still remember the silence as I looked at the benches lining the walls on both sides leaving the center wide open.

I chose a seat halfway down the left side and tried to tell myself that all was well and all I had to do was to be patient and wait.

The door opened and a young man came over to me and said, "Wanna come out and sit in my truck?"

I said, "No, I don't."

He kept it up, getting more persistent saying, "It's nice and warm in my truck, come on."

I said, "No, I don't want to go anywhere, leave me alone."

Suddenly a loud voice said, "Leave the girl alone and be on your way, buddy."

The man and I looked in amazement across the room to see a "big" soldier seated on the opposite bench. I don't know where he came from. He was definitely too big a guy to have missed. Still, I was thanking God under my breath that he was there.

The man glared at the soldier and then told him to mind his own business (along with a few other remarks I would rather not repeat). The soldier looked him straight in the eye, and this time in a commanding voice repeated, "Leave the girl alone, and be on your way, NOW!"

The young man swore but obeyed, storming out the door. When I turned to thank the soldier, he was gone. Gone where? I knew he didn't go out the door. Why was he even there if he wasn't waiting on a train in the middle of the night and in the middle of nowhere?

The rude man sat in his trunk honking the horn for awhile, and finally drove off. My train came and as I boarded I took a last look around. There was no soldier, so how could I ever thank him?

Physically and mentally exhausted, I dozed until the conductor called out, "Poughkeepsie, all out for Poughkeepsie." It was music to my ears! I was lucky to find a taxi outside the station to take me to the hospital. Safe at last in my room, I gave thanks to God and the soldier angel He sent to protect a lonely, frightened girl on a cold winter night.

—*Dona M. Maroney*

Someone to Watch Over Me

*I*n 1949, my high school friend, Louann, and I went to a Friday night movie in Tacoma, Washington. The film was playing at the Community Theater on 56th and Main. After enjoying a night of fun, Louann and I headed out of the theater to begin our 20-block walk back to my house.

Out of the blue, two very frightening, rough-looking men appeared on the darkened, quiet street. They began trailing us, and, of course, we were terribly frightened! We began running as quickly as we could while the two men were following our every move. We went through yards, around corners and even attempted to knock on someone's door, while all the while, the two men were close at hand. The people inside the house were home, but refused to let us in!

We began praying, "God, please help us!"

With nothing left to do but continue running, we scurried down the road, fearing for our lives. Suddenly, a car appeared on the side of the road with two kind-looking young men, one of them inside and the other was standing along side the car. It was as if they were waiting for us. The man outside the car said, "Get in, we know you are in trouble, we'll take you home."

Being girls of a young age during a time when it was not quite so unusual to accept a ride from strangers, and not having any other options available to us at that moment, we cautiously got in. The men seemed to know exactly where I lived, and without asking for directions, took us straight to my house. Upon exiting their vehicle, we thanked them for helping us during what we were certain, had been a life threatening experience. Their only response was, "Do not be afraid."

We proceeded to the door of my house, feeling incredibly grateful to be home and alive. I took out my house key, and both Louann and I thought to turn around one more time, and look at the men who had saved us. Oddly enough, there was simply no trace of them or their car! They had vanished completely into thin air. We did not hear their car drive away nor could we see it traveling down the road in either direction.

I am confident that these two men had not been men at all, but rather angels. They had appeared on a darkened street seemingly out of no where when we needed them the most, and driven us home to safety.

Perhaps not coincidentally, on the very same night in the very same town, my mother had gone out as well, traveling on the city bus line she so often used. After getting off, the bus, someone knocked her down and attempted to attack her on the darkened Tacoma street. When all attempts failed to rescue herself from this man, a mysterious car pulled up and the would-be attacker ran away. She was shaken, but all right. The people in the car never got out of their vehicle, but simply drove away after seeing that she was okay.

Could it be that the same angels who helped Louann and I on that dark night so long ago, also aided my own mother on the very same evening? We will never know, of course, but in my mind, they are the same, and they were most definitely our very own, guardian angels.

—Shirl Ahlquist

Unbeliev-a-bull

On a winter day when I was about 9, I was out checking the cows with my father. One of the bulls had gotten into the wrong pasture and we needed to move him before he caused any unwanted pregnancies. He was an old bull who was usually very calm and compliant, but he refused to be "shooed" by the pickup. He kept going the wrong way.

In an often-used maneuver, my father had me get behind the bull and "shoo" him and keep him going while my father drove his pickup alongside to make sure he went in the right direction. The bull didn't take kindly to a child trying to tell him what to do and turned around and charged me. I stumbled backwards in fear and fell down. I began scrambling backwards and found myself trapped between the charging bull and a very thick mesquite bush. I was so scared that I couldn't even scream. With no place to go, I turned and watch in horror as the bull closed in.

Suddenly, the bull stumbled. He fell down completely and when he tried to get up, he couldn't. He could get his back end up into a standing position, but his head was stuck on the ground. I stayed frozen for a few seconds just watching him try to get his head off of the ground. It was like someone was holding his head down. My father started shouting for me to get up. I did and as soon as I was in the truck, the bull's head was released and he just stood up.

This was the first time I remember really believing in angels.

—Larissa Gardner

Psalm 150

*A*s a professional musician in Nashville, I had been through a lot of things, but once I decided to dedicate my musical ability to the Lord, I had no idea just what kind of opposition I would face from "the other side."

My wife Sherrie (who is a session singer) and I made up our minds to put out a record of original Christian songs. We had already written the material and had a number of professionals ready to get involved. Eager for what was ahead we counted the days until we went to the studio.

Two weeks after getting everything set up, I decided to get some yard work out of the way. One particularly glaring problem was a dying elm tree next to the house. Many elm trees in the area had blight and cutting them down had become a regular chore for me so, with chain saw in hand, I ascended the tree and got ready to get it off of my things to do list.

I began cutting away limbs, working my way to a particularly thick one. As the chain saw chewed into the wood, I worked the cut as I had done hundreds of times before, letting it cut until the weight of the branch started cracking what was left, and then, let it fall.

However, this time, I was surprised as this thick branch suddenly snapped. It turned out it had been rotting inside, and as I cut what little was holding it up, it snapped back, almost as if attacking, throwing me from my perch.

I had the presence of mind to throw the chain saw, but my aim wasn't so good as I actually fell on top of it. It was still running and cut into my face.

As if it were not bad enough being thrown from the tree, and getting sawed, the very branch that knocked me from the tree, came crashing down hard on my leg, badly breaking it.

Sherrie was in the house, and the crashing sounds must have caught her attention. She ran outside, and I can only give credit to God and her faithfulness in Him, because she reached down, and moved the 500 pound limb off of my body. Strong healthy men couldn't have lifted it, but she picked it up and moved it off of me.

The miracle didn't end there though.

The doctor fixed me up but the break was bad and in a bad spot. He said that it would most likely be three months until I would walk again without pain. I hated being sidelined like that.

As I mentioned I am a musician, and among my other pleasures is serving on the church worship team. I play keyboards and guitar mostly, but for this team I primarily played drums. Even with my leg out of commission, I wasn't going to let that stop me from doing what I loved to do, so I put my leg on a chair, and played as best as I could.

The pain was bad, and even more than that, being laid up was putting us in a bind financially too. During one particular service when I was playing, I decided enough was enough and wanted to ask God to fix it. After all, He saved me from being killed by the tree, and the chain saw, *and* He gave my wife the strength to get that limb off of me... why wouldn't He heal me also?

I really felt the Spirit of the Lord was strong in the room that day. While people were in prayer, and asking for prayer, I asked for them to pray for my leg. Practically everyone in the church surrounded me and put their hands on me, each praying for God's healing touch.

As they did this, I began to feel an itching sensation. It was an itch that I knew I couldn't get to because it wasn't outside on the skin, but rather deep inside. I knew the bone was healing right then.

I walked out of the church that day, without crutches and without pain.

The doctors marvelled at the results. They x-rayed my leg, and while the fracture could barely be seen, it had been healed.

I gave glory to God.

Later, at a drugstore, an older woman was looking at crutches, obviously distressed at how much they cost. I remembered I had mine in the truck and gave them to her for free. It was clear to me that God not only took care of me, but put me in a place to give those crutches to someone who needed them more.

Psalm 150 says "Let everything that has breath Praise the Lord," so that is how I end this story, by saying, Praise the Lord!

—*Steve Logan*

He who is a stranger to prayer
is a stranger to power.

When I pray coincidences happen—
and when I don't, they don't.

—William Temple

Do You Have an Angel, Miracle or Inspirational Story?

If you have a story you'd like to share with us, come visit our web site at

www.angelseverywhere.faithweb.com

or you can send us a letter at

Angels Everywhere
Premium Press America
P.O. Box 857,
White House, TN 37188

We look forward to hearing your story!

Premium gift books from PREMIUM PRESS AMERICA include:

I'LL BE DOGGONE
CATS OUT OF THE BAG

STOCK CAR TRIVIA
STOCK CAR GAMES
STOCK CAR DRIVERS & TRACKS
STOCK CAR LEGENDS

GREAT AMERICAN CIVIL WAR
GREAT AMERICAN COUNTRY MUSIC
GREAT AMERICAN GOLF
GREAT AMERICAN OUTDOORS
GREAT AMERICAN STOCK CAR RACING

ANGELS EVERYWHERE
MIRACLES

ABSOLUTELY ALABAMA
AMAZING ARKANSAS
FABULOUS FLORIDA
GORGEOUS GEORGIA
SENSATIONAL SOUTH CAROLINA
TERRIFIC TENNESSEE
TREMENDOUS TEXAS
VINTAGE VIRGINIA

TITANIC TRIVIA
LEONARDO—TEEN IDOL

BILL DANCES FISHING TIPS
DREAM CATCHERS
CLASSIC COOKIES
MILLENNIUM MADNESS

PREMIUM PRESS AMERICA routinely updates existing titles and frequently adds new topics to its growing line of premium gift books. Books are distributed though gift and specialty shops, and bookstores nationwide. If, for any reason, books are not available in your area, please contact the local distributor listed above or contact the Publisher direct by calling 1-800-891-7323. To see our complete backlist and current books, you can visit our website at www.premiumpress.com. Thank you.

Great Reading. Premium Gifts.